BLACK AMERICANS OF DISTINCTION

IMPORTANT BLACK AMERICANS IN
Science and Invention

Don Nardo

San Diego, CA

© 2023 ReferencePoint Press, Inc.
Printed in the United States

For more information, contact:
ReferencePoint Press, Inc.
PO Box 27779
San Diego, CA 92198
www.ReferencePointPress.com

ALL RIGHTS RESERVED.
No part of this work covered by the copyright hereon may be reproduced or used in any form or by any means—graphic, electronic, or mechanical, including photocopying, recording, taping, web distribution, or information storage retrieval systems—without the written permission of the publisher.

LIBRARY OF CONGRESS CATALOGING-IN-PUBLICATION DATA

Names: Nardo, Don, 1947- author.
Title: Important Black Americans in science and invention / by Don Nardo.
Description: San Diego, CA : ReferencePoint Press, 2023. | Series: Black americans of distinction | Includes bibliographical references and index.
Identifiers: LCCN 2022002264 (print) | LCCN 2022002265 (ebook) | ISBN 9781678202880 (library binding) | ISBN 9781678202897 (ebook)
Subjects: LCSH: African American scientists--Juvenile literature. | African American inventors--Juvenile literature.
Classification: LCC Q141 .N23 2023 (print) | LCC Q141 (ebook) | DDC 509.2/396073 [B]--dc23/eng20220318
LC record available at https://lccn.loc.gov/2022002264
LC ebook record available at https://lccn.loc.gov/2022002265

CONTENTS

Introduction — 4
Standing on the Shoulders of Giants

Chapter One — 8
George Washington Carver: Agriculturalist and Inventor

Chapter Two — 18
Percy L. Julian: Chemist and College Professor

Chapter Three — 27
Mae C. Jemison: Physician and Astronaut

Chapter Four — 36
Neil deGrasse Tyson: Astrophysicist and Science Explainer

Chapter Five — 45
Ayana Elizabeth Johnson: Marine Biologist and Conservationist

Source Notes	55
For Further Research	59
Index	61
Picture Credits	64
About the Author	64

INTRODUCTION

Standing on the Shoulders of Giants

The year was 1789. Not long before, in 1776, the thirteen British American colonies had declared their independence and formed a new nation, the United States of America. Among the significant events that occurred in 1789, the representatives of those former colonies met to form a constitution to run the country. Less well-known but still significant, that year also witnessed an American named Benjamin Banneker accurately predict a solar eclipse well before it occurred. Even more remarkable, Banneker, who was not a professional scientist, contradicted and proved wrong the predictions of several noted astronomers. Founding father Thomas Jefferson was so impressed that he later urged the first US president, George Washington, to hire Banneker to help survey the site of the new national capital—Washington, DC.

Banneker's achievements and recognition were also remarkable because of his race. Banneker was Black. He was born near Baltimore, Maryland, in 1731 and lived as a so-called freeman in a time when most Blacks were enslaved. Banneker could never have built his reputation and earned a living as a scientist and inventor if he had been a slave living in drudgery and servitude in the American South. Fortunately for him, Banneker lived in the North, and as a freeman, he could enter any profession he chose.

Still, becoming successful in society at that time was still extremely difficult for non-Whites. This was partly because it was close to impossible for a Black person, even a free one, to acquire a decent education in any profession, especially one as technically oriented as that of a scientist. During the 1700s and early 1800s, colleges were strictly White enclaves that did not accept Black students, who were often dismissed as incapable or unworthy of education. Hence, Banneker and other African Americans of that period were largely self-taught, which made their achievements even more extraordinary.

Embracing Educational Opportunities

At the time, the combination of the institution of slavery and the exclusion of the few Black freemen from schools of higher learning is what kept many more African Americans from becoming scientists and inventors. It was not until 1837 that the first Black college, Cheyney University, was established in Pennsylvania. Initially named the Institute of Colored Youth, it was created by a wealthy White Quaker who believed Black Americans deserved a formal education so that they could become teachers. Only a handful of other such schools appeared—all in the North—before the Civil War (1861–1865). Several more sprang up after that, and Black American scientists and inventors began making their marks on society in greater numbers.

Among these pioneers were several doctors and medical researchers. During the 1860s, for instance, Rebecca Lee Crumpler (born 1831) became the first African American woman to earn a medical degree. She also published a medical text titled *A Book of Medical Discourses.* "I early conceived a liking for, and sought every opportunity to relieve the sufferings of others," she wrote in that volume. In the years following the Civil War, Crumpler cared for thousands of patients in Richmond, Virginia. After that, she later recalled, "I returned to my former home, Boston, where I entered into the work with renewed vigor . . . receiving children in the house for treatment."[1]

It is important to point out that most Black physicians and other scientists were not yet accepted by their white peers or by white society in general. Racism was still strong, even in the North, and Crumpler, a woman, also faced sexism in a male-dominated environment. "Throughout her life, she was ignored, slighted or rendered insignificant," writes newspaper editor Cindy Shmerler. "Because of her race and gender, Crumpler was denied admitting privileges to local hospitals, had trouble getting prescriptions filled by pharmacists, and was often ridiculed by [hospital] administrators and fellow doctors."[2]

Pioneers Who Opened the Way

Nevertheless, Crumpler bravely persevered and continued to benefit her fellow citizens. Other Black scientists and inventors did the same and made key and noteworthy contributions to society. For example, in Chicago in 1893, Daniel Hale Williams became one of the first three US doctors to perform open heart surgery and pioneered certain antiseptic techniques at the same time. Two years before, he had founded Chicago's Provident Hospital, the first

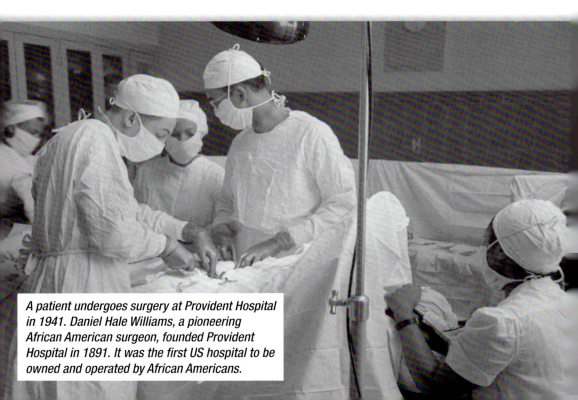

A patient undergoes surgery at Provident Hospital in 1941. Daniel Hale Williams, a pioneering African American surgeon, founded Provident Hospital in 1891. It was the first US hospital to be owned and operated by African Americans.

hospital in the United States to be owned and operated by African Americans.

Meanwhile, Granville Woods, born in 1856, became known as the "Black Edison" for his many technical innovations to emerging technologies such as the telephone and city streetcar. Regarding the latter, he developed the concept of the "third rail" to provide power to the vehicle, an innovation that is still used on subway trains and trolley cars in major cities today. In all, he registered almost sixty US patents for various inventions.

In 1909, a year before Woods's death, African American scientist and explorer Matthew Henson reached the North Pole along with his White and more famous colleague, Robert Perry. Among the young Black people who were inspired by the accomplishments of Henson, Woods, and Williams was Alice A. Ball. Born in 1892, Ball became a chemist in 1915 and soon afterward made the groundbreaking discovery of a successful treatment for the disease leprosy, which had disfigured victims around the world since ancient times. Her younger contemporary, Black physician Charles Drew, made important strides in blood transfusion and created the world's first blood bank.

These and other early pioneers opened the way for the more famous Black scientists to come, including astronaut Mae C. Jemison and astrophysicist and science popularizer Neil deGrasse Tyson. In a television interview in 2016, Tyson acknowledged the debt he and other scientists—both Black and White—owed to those hardworking forerunners. "Each generation benefits from what previous generations have learned," he pointed out. "Isaac Newton, my man, said, 'If I have seen farther than others, it's by standing on the shoulders of giants.'"[3] Tyson and other modern Black scientists and inventors recognize and point to the debt they owe the people who came before them, many of whom struggled against great odds to offer their gifts to the nation and the world.

> "Each generation benefits from what previous generations have learned."[3]
>
> —Neil deGrasse Tyson, astrophysicist

CHAPTER ONE

George Washington Carver: Agriculturalist and Inventor

"By reason of its superior food value, the peanut has become almost a universal diet for man," African American scientist George Washington Carver stated in 1916. He went on, "I do not know of any one vegetable that has such a wide range of food possibilities." Two years later, he said, "Of all the money crops grown by southern farmers, perhaps there is none more promising than the peanut, which can be easily and cheaply grown."[4]

Despite these public expressions of praise for the peanut, Carver, who was fifty-two years old in 1916, was not yet an internationally known scientist and household name. Nor had he yet acquired the popular nickname "Mr. Peanut." Such widespread fame did not come until after January 1921, when he testified before a US congressional committee. That event came about because the main peanut growers in the American South had recently heard about Carver's experiments with peanuts. In 1919, their representative visited Carver in his lab at the Tuskegee Institute (renamed Tuskegee University in 1985) in Alabama. According to one of Carver's leading biographers, the man was "dazzled by both Carver and his many peanut products"[5] and concluded that Carver's work would greatly boost the US peanut industry.

As a result, the soft-spoken Black scientist quickly gained favor among the southern peanut growers. And in 1921 they turned to him for help. They sought to lobby Congress to protect their profits by placing a tax on foreign-grown peanuts and decided that Carver would be their most effective spokesman. When the congressmen, who were all White, heard that an upcoming witness was Black, they made a mistaken assumption based on common racial biases of that era. Figuring he would be an uneducated grower, they allotted him only ten minutes to speak. When Carver began addressing them, however, they quickly realized their error. Transfixed by his highly authoritative manner and striking command of complex facts, they repeatedly extended his time. Moreover, when he finished his testimony, they gave him a round of applause, an honor rarely afforded even to White witnesses by such committees.

Thereafter, Carver swiftly gained recognition in scientific circles both in America and abroad. Although he regularly worked with a wide array of foodstuffs, many people came to associate him primarily with the topic of his testimony—peanuts. On many occasions he corrected people who thought he had invented the peanut or peanut butter. Neither was true, he said. Instead, he reminded them, he had found some three hundred ways to use peanuts, among them making pancake flour, providing meat substitutes, and using them in chicken feed, rubbing oil, shampoo, glue, and metal polish.

> "Of all the money crops grown by southern farmers, perhaps there is none more promising than the peanut."[4]
>
> —George Washington Carver

Childhood and Education

George Washington Carver's eventful journey from slave to world-renowned scientist and inventor began shortly before the close of the American Civil War. The exact year of his birth is somewhat uncertain, but he held, as do most of his biographers, that it was

1864. In contrast, the place and circumstances are not in dispute. His mother, Mary Carver, was a slave owned by Moses Carver, who had a farm in the town of Diamond, Missouri. (It was customary for slaves to take their masters' last names.) Moses allowed Mary to have a family with a slave named Giles, from a neighboring farm. The couple had several children, including George; his older brother, James; and three older sisters, two of whom died before George was born.

When George was only a few weeks old, his father died in a farming accident. Only days later, White raiders from nearby Arkansas kidnapped George, along with his mother and surviving sister, and Moses Carver hired an agent to track them down. The pursuer was able to rescue only George, however. (The fates of Mary and her daughter remain unknown to this day.) After the rescue, Moses and his wife, Susan, freed George and James and thereafter raised them as their own sons.

George later recalled that "Mr. and Mrs. Carver were very kind to me and I thank them so much for my home training." He added that "they encouraged me to secure knowledge, helping me all they could." This may at least partly explain why young George displayed such a passion for learning throughout his life. As a boy, he was particularly fascinated by nature and thereafter never ceased in his desire to understand how it worked. "From a child I had an inordinate desire for knowledge," he later said.

> Day after day I spent in the woods alone in order to collect [flowers] and put them in my little garden [near] my house. . . . Strange to say, all sorts of vegetation seemed to thrive under my touch until I was [given the nickname of] the "plant doctor," and plants from all over the country[side] would be brought to me for treatment. At this time I had never heard of botany and could scarcely read.[6]

Fortunately for young George, Susan Carver taught him to read, which marked the beginning of his formal education. He looked forward to going to school, but as he later reminisced, "no colored schools were available"[7] in his town. Undaunted, he attended a small grammar school for Black children in the neighboring town of Neosho. Later, at age fifteen, he moved to Minneapolis, Kansas, where he lived with a friendly White family, the Seymours, and attended the local high school. Although the students were mostly White, he was accepted and well treated because the Seymours and most of their neighbors believed that African Americans deserved to be educated.

After graduating from high school, Carver was eager to go to college. He applied by mail to Highland College in Highland, Kansas, and thanks to his good grades, was accepted. But the

Scientist George Washington Carver is renowned for his research on peanuts. He was able to find hundreds of uses for peanuts and, in the process, helped to revolutionize southern agriculture.

Carver, Peanut Oil, and Polio

In his extensive research of peanuts, Carver developed various versions of peanut oil, including some that could be used as skin creams and rubbing oils. He came to suspect that one rubbing compound in which peanut oil was the main ingredient might help cure the crippling disease polio, or at least lessen its painful symptoms. To that end, during the 1930s he began to give selected polio victims peanut oil massages. Several of them said that they felt somewhat better afterward, which he and several polio patients viewed as encouraging. Eventually the president of the United States, Franklin D. Roosevelt, who himself suffered from polio, heard about Carver's massages. Roosevelt tried the peanut oil compound and wrote to Carver, saying, in part, "I do use peanut oil from time to time and I am sure that it helps." Regrettably for polio sufferers, it turned out that Carver's massaging oil itself was not an effective treatment for polio. Medical researchers studied the oil and its effects closely and concluded that the massages made patients feel better because a person's muscles always feel better for a while after a massage.

Quoted in Georgia State Parks, "George Washington Carver: Peanut Oil and Polio," *Little White House Newsletter: African Americans, FDR, and Warm Springs*, Winter 2019. https://gastateparks.org.

administrators assumed he was White. And when he showed up to register, they told him he was not welcome because the school did not accept Blacks.

Upset about the rejection, Carver worked for a while on a farm and then, in 1890, tried a different school—Simpson College in Iowa. Run by progressive Methodists, it did accept some African American students, including Carver. At first, he studied art because he had already displayed a great deal of talent as a painter. But one of the professors at Simpson learned of the young man's equally keen aptitude for science and convinced him to major in botany.

Carver the Teacher

After college, Carver decided to pursue a career as an agricultural researcher and teacher. Luckily for him, Booker T. Washington, founder of the Black college the Tuskegee Institute, was looking for someone to run the school's agricultural department. Impressed by Carver's expertise in botany and professional manner, Washington offered him a large salary and free use of a two-room apartment on campus.

Under Carver's effective leadership, Tuskegee's agricultural department thrived and expanded. He had his students follow his lead in researching and developing ways to improve crop rotation and thereby produce bigger harvests. Carver also sought to develop alternative cash crops for farmers in regions where only cotton was grown. Harsh weather conditions and the destruction of cotton crops by the insidious boll weevil had caused much devastation in those areas, and the new approaches Carver championed helped many farmers—Black and White alike—survive and prosper.

Also notable was Carver's use of an outreach program to help and teach farmers in person. Called the Jesup Agricultural Wagon, its use began in rural Alabama in 1906. According to Alabama A&M University communications officer Wendi Williams,

> It was a mobile classroom that allowed Carver to teach farmers and sharecroppers how to grow crops, such as sweet potatoes, peanuts, soybeans and pecans. The wagon's name originates from Morris Jesup, a New York banker who financed the project. However, it was Carver himself who designed the wagon, selected the equipment and developed the lessons for farmers. The earlier model was a horse drawn carriage that was later replaced by a mobile truck. Regardless of how it ran, this successful outreach model was later widely adopted by the United States Department of Agriculture.[8]

Carver the Inventor

During his long tenure at Tuskegee, Carver also experimented extensively with peanuts, soybeans, and other foodstuffs and invented numerous ways to alter and use them. His widely advertised three hundred forms of and uses for the peanut included adding it to salad oil, evaporated milk, instant coffee, laxatives, leather dyes, shaving cream, and printer's ink, and employing it as a castor oil substitute and as a wood filler, among other things. It is important to point out that when Carver listed these three hundred uses, he did not claim to have originated all of them. Some, especially those having to do with candies containing peanuts, already existed, but he listed them to educate the public on the many uses of the peanut. He sometimes patented the uses he invented, including those used in cosmetics and rubbing oils.

The fact that Carver did not get patents for all his inventions reflects his disinterest in marketing products and getting rich from them. Instead, his main intent was to do new research that would educate and benefit members of society. Evidence also suggests that he thoroughly enjoyed his work, especially his experiments with peanuts. In his later years, he joked, "When I was young, I said to God, 'God, tell me the mystery of the universe.' But God answered, 'That knowledge is for me alone.' So I said 'God, tell me the mystery of the peanut.' Then God said, 'Well George, that's more nearly your size.' And he told me."[9]

Meanwhile, in addition to his work with peanuts, Carver found 118 uses for and products derived from sweet potatoes. Among them were multiple flours for making bread, a kind of molasses, a type of vinegar, a glue for postage stamps, a form of artificial rubber, and a kind of gasoline. He also researched or listed some seventy-five products made from pecans.

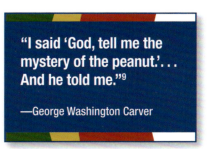

"I said 'God, tell me the mystery of the peanut.'... And he told me."[9]

—George Washington Carver

Little known to the public, Carver's inventiveness gained the attention of the great automobile innovator Henry Ford. As explained by the editors of History.com,

> Ford and Carver began corresponding via letter in 1934, and their mutual admiration deepened after Carver made a visit to [Dearborn] Michigan in 1937.... By the time [the United States entered] World War II [in 1941], Ford had made repeated journeys to Tuskegee to convince Carver to come to Dearborn and help him develop a synthetic rubber to help compensate for wartime rubber shortages. Carver arrived on July 19, 1942, and set up a laboratory in an old water works building in Dearborn. He and Ford experimented with different crops, including sweet potatoes and dandelions, eventually devising a way to make the rubber substitute from goldenrod, a plant weed.[10]

The discovery seemed like a breakthrough, but the arrival of synthetic rubber provided Ford with a cheaper and easier-to-use alternative.

Working Toward Racial Equality

In retrospect, Carver's friendship and work with Ford, a rich White industrialist, well before the civil rights advances of the 1950s and 1960s, may seem surprising. But the truth is that both men respected intelligence, talent, and hard work. Ford strongly believed in equal pay for equal work, regardless of race, and majorly integrated his factories, in time promoting several African Americans to management positions. As for Carver, he was aware of anti-Black racism and the unequal treatment of African Americans, especially in the South. And he wanted to do his part in improving that situation. However, he generally did not involve himself in political speeches, writings, demonstrations, or other overt activism. As a result, pro–civil rights activists—both Black and White—sometimes criticized him for inaction.

But Carver felt that it made more sense for him to approach the problems of race relations in ways that he and his talents could do the most good. He firmly believed that his work in the agricultural sector would help poorer farmers, both Black and

White, make more money and enter the mainstream of American society. That would, he advocated, at least indirectly contribute to better race relations in the country.

Also, Carver recognized that most anti-Black prejudice was based on the simple but potentially powerful emotions fear and hate. "We cry peace," he told a friend in 1931. "There is no permanent peace where . . . [the] races hate each other."[11] The main question, he thought, was how to eliminate that hate. His answer, which today many people would view as overly simplistic, was to urge people to see the benefit of doing the right thing. If only all Americans could "just understand that the Golden Rule way of living is the only correct method, and the only Christ-like method," he stated, "this will settle all of our difficulties that bother us."[12]

His Death and Legacy

Carver's call for all Americans to follow the Golden Rule came shortly before the fateful date of January 5, 1943. On that day, as seventy-eight-year-old Carver was getting ready to leave his apartment at Tuskegee to go to his lab, he tripped and fell down the stairs. He passed away later that day, and soon afterward his friends and students buried him beside the grave of Booker T. Washington on the Tuskegee grounds. They carved a fitting epitaph on Carver's headstone: "He could have added fortune to fame, but caring for neither, he found happiness and honor in being helpful to the world."[13]

Major tributes to Carver were not long in coming. Future president Harry S. Truman, then a Missouri state senator, sponsored a bill in the state legislature to erect a monument to one of the most prominent African Americans of that era. The bill passed unanimously and the monument—a bust of Carver—was finished and dedicated a few years later. In the decades that followed, many schools were named after Carver, along with two US military ships, including the missile submarine USS *George Washington Carver*, which launched in 1965.

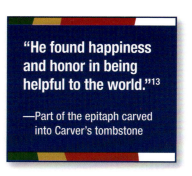

"He found happiness and honor in being helpful to the world."[13]

—Part of the epitaph carved into Carver's tombstone

The First National Monument to an African American

In 1943, Missouri's state legislature passed a bill sponsored by Senator Harry S. Truman to create a monument to honor George Washington Carver. When sculptor Audrey Corwin completed the bust of the scientist, it became the first national memorial to an African American in US history. The George Washington Carver National Monument, situated near Diamond, Missouri, was formally dedicated on July 13, 1953. Later, a nine-foot-high (3 m) bronze statue depicting Carver as a boy, fashioned by sculptor Robert Amendola, was added and dedicated on July 17, 1960. Incorporated into the national monument is the land on which it rests, the 240 acres (97 ha) that originally made up the farm of Carver's adoptive father, Moses Carver. There, George Washington Carver had been born, lived with his mother until her kidnapping, and was later raised by Moses and Susan Carver. At first, the visitor's center at the site was modest in size and scope. In 2007, however, the National Park Service built a new and expanded center covering some 18,000 square feet (1,672 sq. m). It features a museum, theater, gift shop, classrooms, interactive exhibit areas, a library, and a large multipurpose section sometimes used as a tornado shelter.

These and other posthumous honors for Carver were accompanied by speeches that credited him not only with bettering society through his research and experiments but also frequently mentioned how his life symbolized the potential of education, decency, and hard work to transform someone born into difficult circumstances into a model citizen. Carver had once summarized the part played by simple human decency, saying, "How far you go in life depends on your being tender with the young, compassionate with the aged, sympathetic with the striving, and tolerant of the weak and strong. Because someday in your life you will have been all of these."[14]

CHAPTER TWO

Percy L. Julian: Chemist and College Professor

One day in 1939, the telephone in the home of African American chemist Percy L. Julian rang. He had taken a couple of days off from his job as a researcher at the Glidden chemical company in Chicago to spend some time with his wife and wondered who was calling him. It turned out to be one of his assistants at the Glidden plant, where he and his team had been trying to make useful products from soybeans. "Doctor, something has happened," the man told Julian. "Some water leaked into [our] 100,000-gallon tank of soybean oil . . . [and the] oil is spoiled." Clearly concerned, Julian said, "Spoiled? What do you mean?" The assistant replied, "It's full of white solids [that are] floating around in it and settling down on the bottom."[15]

After hurrying to the plant, Julian examined the white solids that had formed during the lab accident and suddenly realized, to his delight, that the mishap had been a blessing in disguise. "Sometimes miracles happen," he told an interviewer years later. Such "accidents characterize the development of science so often," he added. According to a booklet published in 1999 by the American Chemical Society,

Julian realized that the extremely small amounts of sterols [essential chemical components of cell membranes] contained in soybean oil had been concentrated and isolated in the white solids. Subsequent modification of this "accidental procedure" led to the daily production of 100 pounds of mixed soybean sterols worth more than $3.6 million annually. These sterols were then easily converted using methods and equipment designed by Julian to produce commercial quantities of a variety of sex hormones, including progesterone, all at a greatly reduced cost to the public but still with a healthy profit for Glidden.[16]

In addition to progesterone, Julian and his assistants also produced the important male sex hormone testosterone from soybeans. The ability to create large quantities of these hormones in a reasonably simple manner helped to bring about a host of medical advances and treatments. Because of this breakthrough and Julian's many other achievements in the laboratory, he eventually gained recognition as one of the leading chemists of the twentieth century.

A Brilliant, Diligent Student

Percy Lavon Julian was born on April 11, 1899, in Montgomery, Alabama. The grandson of former slaves, he attended segregated schools that enrolled only Black students and ended with the eighth grade. At the time, Alabama had no high schools open to African American youth.

During his eight years of schooling, Julian had shown himself to be a driven student, thirsty for learning, and he desired to continue his education by going to college. So, he applied to DePauw University in Greencastle, Indiana, which had begun accepting Black students in 1882. Because Julian had not gone to high school, he had to take high school–level classes in the evening for several months in order to catch up to the other members of his college classes. A brilliant, diligent student, he not only caught up but also

Growing Up Under "Jim Crow"

Noted African American chemist Percy L. Julian was born in Montgomery, Alabama, in 1899. At the time, people in the American South lived under "Jim Crow," a social system that forced the segregation of Whites and Blacks and maintained strict White supremacy. One of the main hallmarks of Jim Crow was that African Americans consistently feared for their very lives. If a Black person made the wrong remark in public or drank from a water fountain designated for Whites only, he or she might be beaten or even killed. Julian learned of the dangers Blacks faced early in his life, later recalling,

> When I was 12 years old, I went berry-picking on my grandfather's farm in Alabama . . . [and suddenly] came across a Negro body hanging from a tree. He had been lynched a few hours earlier. He didn't look like a criminal; he just looked like a scared boy. On the way back, I encountered and killed a rattlesnake. . . . Many years later, a reporter asked me what were my greatest nightmares from my childhood in the South. I told him, "White folks and rattlesnakes."

Quoted in *NOVA*, "Forgotten Genius," Public Broadcasting Service, February 6, 2007. www.pbs.org.

ended up surpassing all his classmates. He graduated first in his class in 1920, having earned a bachelor's degree in chemistry.

During the next two years, Julian taught organic chemistry at Nashville's Fisk University, a Black college that had been established in 1865. Then he won a scholarship to Harvard University in Cambridge, Massachusetts, where he quickly earned his master's degree. After that, he taught chemistry again, this time at another noted Black college, Howard University in Washington, DC.

Although an African American man with a master's degree in chemistry was considered extraordinary in that era, Julian was still not satisfied. He was strongly motivated to get his doctorate

(PhD), and to that end, he earned a fellowship to study from 1929 to 1931 at the University of Vienna in Austria. At the time, it had one of the world's leading chemistry departments.

A World-Class Achievement

Armed with his doctorate from Vienna, Julian returned to Washington, DC, where he had been hired to teach at Howard University once more. There, he met and courted Anna Roselle, who had a PhD in sociology from the University of Pennsylvania. Eventually, the couple married and had two children—Percy Jr., born in 1940, and Faith, born in 1944.

Having taught at Howard for only a year, in 1932 Julian accepted an offer to both teach part-time and do lab research at his alma mater, DePauw. That research was mainly concerned with the chemical properties of plants and the medicines and other useful substances that could possibly be made from them. He was convinced that such chemicals could potentially help millions of people around the world lead better, healthier lives.

It did not take long for Julian to create such a substance. In 1935, working with Josef Pikl, a colleague he had met and befriended in Vienna, Julian succeeded in synthesizing, or artificially creating in a lab, a key chemical found in Calabar beans. As explained in the acclaimed 2007 Public Broadcasting Service (PBS) television documentary on Julian's life,

> Chemists had been fascinated by the Calabar bean ever since British missionaries brought it back from Africa in the mid-1800s. From the bean, they had isolated an alkaloid called physostigmine—used to treat [the serious eye ailment] glaucoma—but no one had been able to synthesize the complex molecule. . . . Synthesis was the highest calling for a chemist in the 1930s. A successful synthesis could bring great medical benefits, by making a scarce natural product more widely available. Just as important, it proved beyond a doubt that the chemist understood how the molecule was put together.[17]

Through his research, chemist Percy Julian hoped to find many uses for soybeans, but a lab accident led in a direction he never expected. He developed ways to create large quantities of the sex hormones progesterone and testosterone for a variety of medical needs.

The synthesis of physostigmine from Calabar beans was widely hailed as a major scientific achievement, and it earned Julian recognition and congratulations from chemists and other scientists around the globe. He was sure that this accomplishment would be enough to persuade DePauw's administrators to make him a full-time professor. But he was wrong. Despite his world-class achievement, racism was then still extremely prevalent in the United States, and his superiors refused to promote him, telling him to his face that it was because he was Black.

Early Career Successes

This was not the first time that Julian had encountered the barriers of racial inequality. Nor was it the last. Indeed, hoping to land a job at a private company, away from the academic arena, he applied to several well-known chemical companies. However, the first reactions he received were both disappointing and disheartening. He later remembered, "Day by day, as I entered these firms, presented my credentials and asked for a job, the answer almost seemed like it had been transmitted by wire from one firm to the other. It ran like this: 'We've never hired a Negro research chemist before. We don't know how it would work out.'"[18]

> "As I entered these firms, presented my credentials and asked for a job, the answer [was always no]."[18]
>
> —Percy Julian

After several months of such rejections, however, Julian's fortunes took a major turn for the better. An Irish businessman named William J. O'Brien, who knew about Julian's work with the Calabar bean, heard that he was looking for a job. O'Brien, vice president of the Glidden chemical firm, was searching for a gifted chemist to run the company's new Chicago lab. Smart enough to know that skin color has nothing to do with intelligence or talent, early in 1936 he offered Julian the position of director of research in that division of the company.

It swiftly became evident that O'Brien had made the right decision in hiring Julian. During the late 1930s, the new lab director led his team of assistants in making a series of groundbreaking discoveries and inventions in plant-based chemistry. One such invention was the development of Aer-O-Foam, which derived from Julian's studies of the complex molecule making up soy protein. Aer-O-Foam, which was highly effective at putting out oil and gas fires, soon saw wide use by the military during World War II. The lab also invented a special glue that enabled plywood to be made inexpensively from Douglas fir. These discoveries both benefited the country and its economy and helped Glidden expand.

Julian and the Cortisone Production Race

In the later years of his prolific career—during the 1940s and 1950s—Julian continued to make important scientific advances that further solidified his reputation as one of the greatest living chemists. Initially, these achievements, many in the area of synthesizing hormones, continued to be made at the Glidden facility. But eventually the Glidden executives decided they no longer wanted to produce hormone-related products, which prompted Julian to leave and start his own company.

To a large degree, these events were driven by Julian's groundbreaking work in the historic effort to synthesize hydrocortisone (often simply called *cortisone*), a hormone made in the human adrenal glands. In 1949 medical researchers at the famous Mayo Clinic in Rochester, Minnesota, found that cortisone is very effective in treating rheumatoid arthritis, a painful inflammation of the joints. According to a young, popular rheumatologist (joint disease doctor) of that era, the late Charles Plotz, "Every patient with rheumatoid arthritis immediately wanted to be put on this magic drug."[19]

But that was not possible at the time. One problem was that obtaining a mere gram of cortisone was extremely difficult and expensive. Some scientists studying the chemical found that it could be derived from the livers of cattle. However, that required a complex sixteen-step process; hence, as Plotz pointed out, thousands of cattle would need to be slaughtered in order to make enough cortisone to treat a single human patient. "I would get requests from all over the country," he said. "'Can't you get me some cortisone? Can't you get a little cortisone for me? For my aunt? For my patient?' And I couldn't get it, for me or for anybody."[20] Clearly, someone needed to find a way to synthesize cortisone in an easier, less expensive manner.

Beginning in mid-1949, chemists in labs around the world, including Percy Julian, raced to find such a way. Late that year, Julian announced that he had solved a major part of the problem. From soybean oil, he had managed to create a chemical that came to be widely known as Substance S. It was identical to cortisone except that Substance S's molecule had one less oxygen atom than cortisone. Some researchers at a rival company, Upjohn, found a way to insert an extra oxygen atom into Substance S. Upjohn's lab also found a way to convert progesterone, the sex hormone that Julian had created in quantity in 1939, into cortisone.

Julian Explains His Work with Soybean Protein

When Percy Julian began working at Glidden in 1936, his first assignment was to work on exploiting the chemical properties of the soybean plant. He later recalled the project, saying,

> We dared to do something rather bold. We thought we would isolate [soybean] protein, pure. And I built a plant for isolating this protein from the soybean, the first venture that had been attempted in history to prepare a pure vegetable protein by isolating it from a plant. Fifty percent of the weight of the soybean is protein. And what a protein! No other protein that we've known [is so similar to] the basic protein of animals and humans as soybean protein. And we did isolate this protein from the soybean. [At first we] produced five tons a day. Some few years later that was increased to 10 tons, and then, by the time I left the Glidden Company, to 15 tons a day. I called yesterday to find out actually how much was being produced daily now in this plant, and they're producing 50 tons of pure soy protein a day now from this plant.

Quoted in *NOVA*, "Julian Speaks," Public Broadcasting Service, 2007. www.pbs.org.

Thus, two major substances pioneered by Julian now rested at the heart of potential large-scale cortisone production. It was a surprise, therefore, not only to Julian but also to chemists everywhere, when in 1953 the Glidden bosses decided to abandon the company's work in hormones. In 1954, Julian reacted by forming his own company—Julian Laboratories, headquartered in Franklin Park, Illinois. Soon it became clear to all the competitors in the hormone production market that larger quantities of hormones such as progesterone could be made from Mexican yams than from soybeans. So, Julian Laboratories built a plant in Mexico, where the company eventually used yams to make synthetic hormones.

A Remarkable List of Accomplishments

When Julian left Glidden to form his own company, he gave up a yearly salary of about $50,000, equivalent to over $500,000 in 2022. Therefore, at the time, he was already a well-to-do individual. Almost eight years later, in 1961, deciding to retire, he sold Julian Laboratories for $2.3 million (equivalent to more than $24 million in 2022), making him one of the few African American millionaires.

In addition to this financial legacy, when he passed away from liver cancer on April 19, 1975, Julian left behind a remarkable list of accomplishments and honors. He was the first Black chemist elected to the National Academy of Sciences, for instance, an accolade he received two years before his death. Also, during his fruitful career he registered some 130 chemistry-related patents. In addition, he received eighteen honorary degrees from various colleges and universities. The National Inventors Hall of Fame inducted him posthumously in 1990, and in 1999 the American Chemical Society recognized his synthesis of physostigmine from Calabar beans as one of the twenty-five greatest feats in the history of American chemistry.

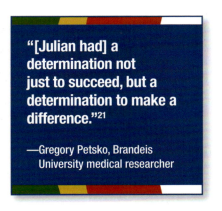

"[Julian had] a determination not just to succeed, but a determination to make a difference."[21]

—Gregory Petsko, Brandeis University medical researcher

Moreover, chemists and other scientists have repeatedly pointed out that Julian amassed these astonishing achievements mostly during a period in which racism made it extremely difficult for talented Black people to succeed in American society. In the words of Brandeis University medical researcher Gregory Petsko, Julian constantly "had to overcome the disadvantages of his race. [Yet] looking over his life, one has a sense that here is a man of great determination. And it's a determination not just to succeed, but a determination to make a difference, to make a contribution."[21] Noted chemist Gregory Robinson agrees and adds, "For him to have accomplished what he did, with the resources that he had, is still amazing."[22]

CHAPTER THREE

Mae C. Jemison: Physician and Astronaut

In the fall of 1966, ten-year-old Mae Carol Jemison sat mesmerized before the television in her family's first-floor apartment in Chicago's South Side. A new hour-long television series had suddenly caught her attention, as it had done to people of all ages across the nation. Called *Star Trek,* it was set in the mid-twenty-third century and followed the adventures of the crew of a massive star cruiser, the USS *Enterprise.*

For young Jemison, the show seemed like icing on a cosmic cake she had already begun to eagerly devour. In the preceding year, she had developed an intense love of science, particularly topics having to do with the stars, planets, and space travel. "I already knew that I would [someday] travel in space," she recalled as an adult. "I had a set of encyclopedias that gave the step by step details of how a human would arrive on the surface of the moon. I had latched onto the study of how the universe began, how stars were formed, how life began and evolved on Earth, and the future colonization of other planets as a lifelong interest."[23]

Star Trek therefore fell directly into Jemison's area of interest. One aspect of the show that she especially liked was that the ship's crew was diverse, comprising people

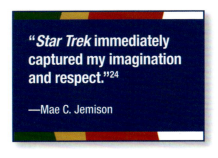

"*Star Trek* immediately captured my imagination and respect."[24]

—Mae C. Jemison

of both genders, different races and ethnic groups, and even beings from other worlds. "Wow!" she thought at the time, "somewhere, someone else believed that other kinds of people would populate spaceships from Earth." Also, the show "presented a hopeful view of humanity and the future." For those and other reasons, Jemison later said, "*Star Trek* immediately captured my imagination and respect."[24]

Most of all, Jemison was impressed with and inspired by the *Enterprise*'s chief communications officer, an African American woman named Lieutenant Uhura. "She was the first woman to appear regularly on television in a technical role," Jemison later wrote. "She was intelligent, skilled, gorgeous, cool, and looked a bit like me and the women around me."[25] So enamored was Jemison with Uhura that the girl became more determined than ever to go into space herself someday. The youngster's introduction to *Star Trek* proved to be one of the major turning points of her life. Jemison did, in fact, eventually become an astronaut with the National Aeronautics and Space Administration (NASA)—and the first Black woman in space. She also met and became close friends with Nichelle Nichols, the actor who portrayed Uhura. To honor her fictional role model, while in Earth orbit during the 1990s, Jemison began all her messages to NASA's mission control with Uhura's signature line: "Hailing frequencies open."[26]

Childhood and Early Schooling

The future first female African American astronaut was born on October 17, 1956, in Decatur, Alabama. The third child of Dorothy and Charlie Jemison, young Mae had two siblings—an older brother, Ricky, and an older sister, Ada. When she was four, her family moved to Chicago, where they flitted from apartment to apartment for a while before landing permanently in one on the South Side.

One of Jemison's most vivid memories of that period was her mother's determination to better herself, a recollection that in-

Reuniting the Arts and Sciences

In 2002, Jemison gave a technology, entertainment, design (TED) talk. In that lecture, she made the case that science and the arts are closely related because they both require a certain amount of creativity. She stated, in part,

> What is our mission [as modern humans]? What do we have to do? I think our mission is to reconcile [reunite] science and the arts. . . . People have this idea that science and the arts are really separate. . . . If we keep thinking that [way] . . . then we're going to have problems. . . . By accepting this dichotomy [separation] we're messing up the future. . . . [The truth is that] the creativity that allowed us to build and launch the space shuttle springs forth from the same sources, imagination, and analysis it took to carve a [statue] or the ingenuity it took to design, choreograph, and stage [a Broadway show]. Each are different manifestations [of] human creativity, and that's what we have to reconcile in our minds—how these things fit together. . . . They're all part of us. They're all part of a continuum [coherent whole].

Mae Jemison, "Teach Arts and Sciences Together," TED Conferences, February 2002. www.ted.com.

spired the girl more than once over the years. Back when the Jemisons were in Alabama, she later remembered,

> my mother had completed two years of college, but still could only find work cleaning white people's houses. . . . There was little opportunity to complete her degree in Alabama. In Chicago, though, my mother did complete college and then became a schoolteacher. She then went on to get her Master's degree and took up writing as well. . . . I was always so proud that my mother worked, because back then most women did not. I thought she was very special.[27]

As she grew older and went from one Chicago school to another, Jemison excelled at her studies. Convinced she would eventually become a scientist and astronaut, she absorbed information like the proverbial sponge. As a result, in the sixth grade a teacher measured her abilities by giving her a reading test designed for high school seniors. Jemison aced it with ease, and the following year the school placed her in the eighth-grade reading section rather than the seventh-grade one.

High School, College, and a Medical Degree

Jemison next attended Chicago's Morgan Park High School, thereby entering a period during which she was almost constantly busy. Not only did she continue to do exceptionally well in her classwork, but her thirst for learning about astronomy and other aspects of science also led her to frequent the library located roughly a mile from her home. Sometimes, after completing her homework, she would settle into a favorite chair at the library and read for hours. It was not unusual for her to get home at 9:00 p.m. on some weeknights.

While reading her way through the library's science section, Jemison noticed some adult science fiction novels, eagerly read them, and became hooked on that fascinating genre. Some of those novels had been written by scientists, including astronomer Fred Hoyle and chemist Isaac Asimov. Hoyle's *A for Andromeda* and *The Black Cloud* were page-turners for her. Books with space travel themes by "Isaac Asimov and Arthur C. Clarke became staples," she says.

> I started ordering [volumes] from the Science Fiction Book of the Month Club. Why was I hooked? Inside each science fiction book I saw the hope that humans would do better, that we could advance. [I found] mystery and adversity . . . imagination, fantasy, and possibilities between the pages. . . . I identified with the desire to [better] understand the world.[28]

The *Enterprise*'s Only Real Astronaut

In 1993, actor Levar Burton, who played Commander Geordi La Forge on *Star Trek: The Next Generation* (one of the spin-offs of the original series), heard that Mae Jemison was a big *Star Trek* admirer. So, he contacted her and asked if she would like to make a cameo appearance on the show. When she said yes, he arranged it, and that year she appeared briefly as an *Enterprise* crew member—Lieutenant Palmer—in the show's sixth-season episode "Second Chances." A running joke behind the scenes was that although she was on screen for only a few seconds, she had compiled far more spaceflight time than all the members of the ship's crew combined! She also had the distinction of being the first real astronaut to ever appear in a *Star Trek* series. In addition, Jemison later appeared in two TV documentaries about *Star Trek*. One, *Star Trek: 30 Years and Beyond,* aired in 1996; the other, *How William Shatner Changed the World,* appeared in 2005. About her short stint as Lieutenant Palmer, Jemison said, "Everything we do in the world is about imagination and using your creativity to expand beyond your normal boundaries."

Quoted in TrekCore, "Dr. Mae Jemison Interviewed About 'Star Trek' Appearance (1993)," YouTube, March 25, 2018. www.youtube.com/watch?v=UDRJVnja-C0.

Jemison graduated from her high school in 1973 at the age of fifteen. Her teachers and her classmates and their parents were amazed that despite her tender age she had been voted student council president and "most likely to succeed" among the members of the senior class. Having earned straight As throughout her high school career, she also received scholarship offers from colleges across the country, including the Massachusetts Institute of Technology (MIT) in Cambridge and Stanford University near Palo Alto, California.

Jemison selected Stanford. She majored in chemical engineering, but while there, she increasingly gained an interest in medicine and decided to become a doctor. Yet she had not given up on her dream of going into space. Rather, she reasoned that in time NASA would want to send at least one doctor into orbit or to the moon—someone like Dr. McCoy on *Star Trek.* If so, she reasoned, she would be ready to compete for that position. Accordingly, after graduating from Stanford in 1977, she enrolled at Cornell Medical College in New York City. In 1981 she graduated with her medical degree, and the following year she finished her internship at a Southern California medical center.

A Childhood Dream Comes True

Now a trained physician, Jemison treated patients in Los Angeles for a year. Then she became a doctor in the Peace Corps, which took her to the African countries of Liberia and Sierra Leone for

NASA astronaut Mae Jemison became the first Black woman in space in 1992. That year the space shuttle Endeavour *carried Jemison and six other astronauts beyond Earth's atmosphere and into space.*

two years. Returning to America in 1985, she decided it was finally time to attempt to make her childhood dream come true. She knew that during the 1960s and early 1970s NASA had accepted only men—most often test pilots—to train as astronauts. In 1978, however, the space agency had opened its doors to women by accepting Sally Ride to its training program. Ride became the first American woman in space as part of the space shuttle *Challenger* crew in 1983.

Thus, Jemison realized that she had at least a chance of becoming an astronaut and traveling into space. In November 1985, she applied to NASA. A bit more than a year and a half later, the life-changing news came in the form of a phone call. "Is this Dr. Mae Jemison?" a male voice asked. "Yes it is," she answered. "This is George Abbey at NASA and we wanted to know if you still wanted to be an astronaut." When she answered in the affirmative, he added, "Well, we would like you to come on board."[29]

It turned out that Jemison's acceptance had been an even more amazing feat than she had realized at that time. She later found out that she had been one of only fifteen individuals chosen out of more than two thousand applicants. A full year of difficult, demanding training followed. During that period, Jemison studied harder than ever and learned much about the hazards of spaceflight, the space shuttle's technical systems, planetology, geology, and meteorology. She also learned that NASA's choosing her as the first Black female astronaut made an important public statement about the need for both government agencies and society in general to be fair and inclusive. But Jemison knew how hard women and minorities must work to be included. In an article written a decade later by Jesse Katz (who was, at the time, Houston bureau chief for the *Los Angeles Times*), Katz observed that Jemison "is angrier than she once was about how inherently unfair that is, about how impossibly superb members of those excluded groups are expected to be in order to prove that merit, not entitlement, won them an opportunity." Still, Katz added, "without dismissing society's obvious inequities, Jemison

"Without dismissing society's obvious inequities, Jemison remains convinced that the only true limits are the ones we impose on ourselves—or permit others to impose on us."[30]

—Jesse Katz, *Los Angeles Times* Houston bureau chief

remains convinced that the only true limits are the ones we impose on ourselves—or permit others to impose on us."[30]

After her preliminary, general training, Jemison continued learning, now focusing on the experiments she would be conducting while in Earth orbit. NASA wanted her to monitor the crew's health and see how their weeks of spaceflight affected them. This was where her abilities as a physician would come to the fore.

The moment Jemison had been waiting for since her preteen years finally came on September 12, 1992. That day the space shuttle *Endeavour* carried her and six other astronauts aloft and beyond Earth's atmosphere. The craft orbited the planet 126 times before landing at the Kennedy Space Center in Florida on September 20. The flight had lasted 190 hours, 30 minutes, and 23 seconds.

Still Dreaming Big

In the years following the mission, Jemison was frequently asked what it was like and how it felt to be in space. Her answer was almost always like one she gave in an online interview in 2001. In part, she said,

> Being in space has many qualities to it. I was not afraid, I was very excited and happy. The biggest thing is you can look out the window and you can see Earth, and you can see the sun, and you can see the stars, and they are very clear. So that's magical. On the other hand, you can also float around. It's a lot of fun! It feels very different from being on Earth.[31]

Also following her historic flight, Jemison received numerous commendations and awards. They included several honorary doctorates from colleges around the nation, the Ebony Black Achievement Award, and the honor of having a public school in Detroit named after her.

After leaving NASA in 1993, Jemison taught at Dartmouth College in New Hampshire. She also established a company, the Jemison Group. Its goal is to encourage respect for and a love of science in young people in hopes that they will have more fruitful and/or satisfying futures. Looking to her own future, meanwhile, she has said, "My life, I imagine and hope, [will continue] to hold secrets, new challenges, and good times."[32]

Regarding those possible new challenges, Jemison still dreams big. On a number of occasions, she has indicated her desire to somehow travel to Mars or, if at all possible, a planet in an alien solar system. During her brief but life-fulfilling excursion into space, she recalls, "I imagined that I was traveling around a star 10,000 light years away and would never return to Earth. And that felt just fine." Yet even if she is never able to accomplish such mind-boggling voyages, she says, she will have no regrets. In that case, she will simply "devote the remainder of my life to studying the stars and thereby, hopefully, advance human knowledge."[33] These words, along with Jemison's accomplishments, have inspired countless members of later generations. After hearing her speak at the University of Wisconsin in 2020, for example, graduate student Coty Weathersby was moved to say, "She reaffirmed that the stars truly are the limit and you can do anything you set your mind to."[34]

> "My life, I imagine and hope, [will continue] to hold secrets."[32]
>
> —Mae C. Jemison

CHAPTER FOUR

Neil deGrasse Tyson: Astrophysicist and Science Explainer

"It was a dark and starry night,"[35] astrophysicist Neil deGrasse Tyson recalls with an air of longing and fondness. On that night in 1968, nine-year-old Tyson sat inside the Hayden Planetarium in New York City and marveled at the accurate replica of the night sky projected on its ceiling. One thing that was missing was the city's light pollution, which so often marred the boy's observations from the roof of the apartment building in the Bronx where he lived with his parents. Because the planetarium show removed the effects of light pollution, young Tyson could see much more than he normally did from his building. The planetarium show displayed the Big Dipper and Little Dipper, the planets Jupiter and Saturn, the Milky Way, and other sky wonders.

When the house lights came up after the forty-five-minute presentation, Tyson was a forever changed person. "That was the night," he stated years later as an adult scientist.

> That night the universe poured down from the sky and flowed into my body. I had been called. The study of the universe would be my career, and no force on Earth would stop me. I was just nine years

old, but I now had an answer for that perennially annoying question all adults ask: "What do you want to be when you grow up?" Although I could barely pronounce the word, I would tell them, "I want to be an astrophysicist."[36]

A Voracious Reader and Avid Student

The preteen who was so moved by his experience at the Hayden Planetarium and who, in an unexpected twist of fate, would years later become its director, was born in New York City on October 5, 1958. His father, Cyril deGrasse Tyson, was a human resources commissioner for the city, and his mother, Sunchita M. Tyson, was a gerontologist (a scientist who studies aging). The couple had two other children—a son, Stephen, and a daughter, Lynn.

The family made its home in the Castle Hill neighborhood of the Bronx, and as he grew, young Tyson attended Bronx public schools, including the Bronx High School of Science. To get into that specialized school for gifted students, applicants had to pass a three-hour-long exam; some idea of the test's difficulty can be seen in the fact that only about eight hundred of some thirty thousand applicants are accepted each year. The young man not only got into the school and received good grades, but he also distinguished himself by becoming captain of the wrestling team and editor in chief of the student-run *Physical Science Journal.*

> "I had been called. The study of the universe would be my career."[36]
>
> —Neil deGrasse Tyson

Throughout his teenage years, meanwhile, Tyson avidly absorbed knowledge about astronomy as well as physics. Astrophysics, the field he had chosen, is a specialized branch of astronomy that investigates the physical processes that drive the stars, planets, and other objects making up the universe. And he did take courses in those subjects at Bronx Science, as the school was popularly known. But they were too easy for him. So,

Explaining Why "Belief" Has No Place in Science

As a world-renowned science explainer, Tyson has often responded—by letter, email, podcast, or television interview—to questions and comments from nonscientists about how science works. Often, he says, people ask him whether he "believes in" various scientific ideas, and he typically sets them straight about why *belief* is the wrong word choice in scientific matters. To a fan letter that suggested he believes in evolution, he responded, in part, by explaining that

> the theory of evolution is not something to "believe in." Science follows evidence. And when strong evidence supports an idea, the concept of belief, when invoked the way religious people use the word, is unnecessary. In other words, established science is not an ensemble of beliefs, it's a system of ideas supported by verifiable evidence. You did not ask if I believe in the sunrise. Or if I believe the sky is blue. Or if I believe Earth has a moon. These are non-controversial truths about the physical world for which the word "believe" has no place. Evolution by natural selection is a non-controversial tenet of modern biology.

Neil deGrasse Tyson, *Letters from an Astrophysicist*. New York: Norton, 2019, p. 99.

he supplemented them by reading voraciously and by taking astronomy, math, and physics courses offered to the public at the Hayden Planetarium.

One of those courses, titled "Stars, Constellations, and Legends," was taught by astronomer Fred Hess, who lectured in the large chamber beneath the planetarium's dome. Tyson later said that his resonant, echoing voice seemed like a "godlike sound that emanated from the depths of space." At that time, "Hess's course reveled in the majesty and romance of the night sky and reaffirmed for me the simple joys of just looking up. My current lecture manner and style under the dome of the [planetarium's] Sky Theater, and under the canopy of the night sky itself, remain traceable to the talents of Dr. Hess."[37]

A Day with a Renowned Astronomer

After graduating from Bronx Science in 1976, Tyson, then seventeen, applied to five different colleges. His first three choices were Harvard, MIT, and Cornell. Initially, he was almost certain that he would attend Harvard, but then Cornell suddenly seemed like a strong possibility, mainly because of the intervention of Carl Sagan. One of the leading astronomers of the twentieth century, Sagan was then a faculty member at Cornell. "My letter of application [to Cornell] had been dripping with an interest in the universe," Tyson later recalled.

> The admission office, unbeknownst to me, had forwarded my application to Carl Sagan's attention. Within weeks, I received a personal letter inviting me up to Ithaca [New York] to visit him. . . . Carl was warm, compassionate, and demonstrated what appeared to be a genuine interest in my life's path. At the end of the day he drove me back to the Ithaca bus station and jotted down his home phone number—just in case the bus could not navigate through the snow and I needed a place to stay. I never told him this, but at every stage in my scientific career that followed, I have modeled my encounters with students after my first encounter with Carl.[38]

The College Years Fly By

As it turned out, for a variety of personal reasons, Tyson chose to attend Harvard. There, he majored in physics and ravenously consumed as much knowledge as he could. Yet, as he had done in high school, he still managed to find time for extracurricular activities of various sorts. He continued wrestling and joined the rowing crew as well. In addition, he took dancing lessons, including styles as diverse as ballet, jazz, and Latin ballroom.

Perhaps because he was so ceaselessly busy, to him the years seemed to fly by. Before he knew it, 1980 had arrived and he had graduated from Harvard. Next, without missing a proverbial beat, he began his graduate work at the University of Texas in Austin, where he earned a master's degree in astronomy in 1983. While there, he helped pay his way by being a teaching assistant for some of the professors. He was particularly impressed with the quality of the lectures of astronomer Frank N. Bash. "He remains," Tyson later wrote, "the only professor I have ever seen who teaches to the mind of the student and not to the syllabus or the chalkboard. . . . By the end of every introductory astronomy course that he taught, the students knew how to think about the physical world around them."[39] As for Bash, he remembers Tyson with equal affection, saying in part, "Neil had a natural gift for teaching. After he taught, the students would beg for him back."[40]

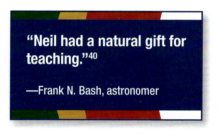

"Neil had a natural gift for teaching."[40]

—Frank N. Bash, astronomer

In 1987, Tyson accepted an offer to lecture in astronomy for two semesters at the University of Maryland. The following year, he began working toward a PhD in astrophysics at New York City's Columbia University. During the nearly three years that followed, his doctoral research gave him access to a large telescope. With the aid of some undergraduate assistants hired by the university, he investigated the formation of stars and galaxies, helping to advance human knowledge of the early universe.

The Rise of a Science Explainer

In the years immediately following the completion of his doctorate, Tyson found himself bombarded by professional offers. Some involved his teaching at the university level, others were requests for him to do research or publish books, and still others called

Astrophysicist Neil deGrasse Tyson (pictured in 2020) has made space science accessible to millions through his books and frequent appearances on radio and television.

on him to head astronomy-related organizations or institutions. In 1994, for instance, he began doing periodic research at Princeton University. And soon afterward he started writing the "Universe" column for *Natural History* magazine.

Perhaps the biggest and most newsworthy position he took during this period was at his old haunt, the Hayden Planetarium. He joined that prestigious institution's staff in 1994, and the following year he was asked to assume the post of director. Not only did he now run the place, but he also oversaw part of its $210 million reconstruction project, which was not completed until 2000. For Tyson, leading the planetarium was, in a sense, a wheel of life that had come full circle. "I never dreamed that I'd be [its] director," he later told an interviewer.

> But now that I am, one of my greatest privileges is signing the certificates of completion for classes taken by youths and adults. I received these same certificates, signed

by the head of the planetarium, when I was a kid taking classes. I see it as a real honor and privilege and duty to serve others in their ambition to become scientists the way scientists and educators served my interest when I was young. To the extent to which it fulfills that goal, my role in the planetarium creates for me a significantly more magnified pleasure in holding the position.[41]

Another consequence of Tyson's decision to head the planetarium was that it thrust him squarely into the public eye. Large numbers of Americans seemed to enjoy his congenial manner and ability to make complex concepts understandable to average people. Thereafter, most of the job offers and honors he received in one way or another involved his being a science explainer for the public, much as scientist-writers Isaac Azimov and Carl Sagan had been. This influenced President George W. Bush's 2001 decision to ask Tyson to join the Commission on the Future of the United States Aerospace Industry. Four years later, for his advancement of the image of science, Tyson received the NASA Distinguished Public Service Medal, the highest civilian honor conferred by NASA.

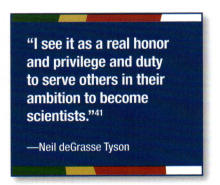

"I see it as a real honor and privilege and duty to serve others in their ambition to become scientists."[41]

—Neil deGrasse Tyson

Tyson also began receiving more and more offers to host television specials and series. In 2004, for example, he hosted a four-part PBS-*NOVA* miniseries titled *Origins,* and a few years later PBS asked him to narrate its popular television documentary *400 Years of the Telescope.* He was also frequently asked to make guest appearances on daily and weekly talk shows, including *The Daily Show, The View,* and *Real Time with Bill Maher.*

In a similar vein, in 2009 Tyson began hosting *StarTalk Radio,* a science-based talk show presented on radio and online. It covered not only scientific topics but also aspects of comedy and popular culture and featured various celebrity cohosts. They and

Why Science Has Become Multidisciplinary

Although he is an astrophysicist, Tyson often finds himself working closely with other kinds of scientists. In a 2004 online interview by the makers of PBS's *NOVA* series, Tyson commented on why science has become multidisciplinary in recent times.

> One thing that distinguishes us today from the discoveries of the past is the extent to which the exploration of the universe has become multidisciplinary. It was unthinkable not long ago that a biologist or paleontologist would be at the same conference as an astrophysicist. Now we have accumulated so much data in each of these branches of science as it relates to origins that we have learned that no one discipline can answer questions of origins alone. It requires the additional insights that one gets by merging not only the questions, but the answers, among scientific disciplines. Now, for example, when you look for life on Mars, you need the astrophysicist to characterize the environment in which the planet is found. You need the chemist to understand the chemistry of the soils. You need the geologist to understand the rock formations. You need the biologist, because no one else will know what life will look like.

Quoted in *NOVA Origins*, "A Conversation with Neil deGrasse Tyson," Public Broadcasting Service, 2004. www.pbs.org.

Tyson interviewed well-known guests, including actors Morgan Freeman and George Takei, the late stand-up comic Joan Rivers, and noted evolutionary biologist Richard Dawkins. The show proved so popular that it spawned a television version that premiered in 2015.

Tyson reached an even larger audience when, in 2014, he edited and hosted the thirteen-episode television series *Cosmos: A Spacetime Odyssey*. It was inspired by Carl Sagan's classic thirteen-episode science documentary, *Cosmos,* first broadcast in 1980. (In an episode of the new series, Tyson was careful to include a brief, respectful reenactment of his personal interaction with Sagan back in the late 1970s.) The updated version of *Cosmos* had an audience numbering in the millions and was nominated for twelve Emmy Awards. Summing up Tyson's abilities as a science explainer, Bill Prady, cocreator of the popular television show *The Big Bang Theory,* said, "Someone like Neil comes on television, he's friendly, he's funny, he's a good teacher. More people like him would represent a positive shift in the culture."[42]

At One with the Universe

Amazingly, despite this seemingly endless flurry of activities, Tyson periodically found the time to write books. Among the more popular have been *Astrophysics for People in a Hurry* (2017), *Letters from an Astrophysicist* (2019), and *A Brief Welcome to the Universe* (2021). In promotional interviews for the latter book, Tyson was often asked what plans he had for the future. More than once he answered that he expected to keep trying to solve the riddles of the universe until he becomes one with it. And he meant that quite literally. In his semibiographical book *The Sky Is Not the Limit* (2000)*,* he writes, "We are not simply *in* the universe; we are a part of it." When he dies, Tyson explains, he wants to be buried, not cremated.

> The least I can do is donate my body back to this third rock from the Sun. I want to be buried, just like in the old days, where I decompose by the action of microorganisms, and I am dined upon by any form of creeping animal, or root system that sees fit to do so. I would become their food, just as they had been food for me. I will have recycled back to the universe at least some of the energy that I have taken from it. And in so doing, at the conclusion of my scientific adventures, I will have come closer to the heavens than to earth.[43]

CHAPTER FIVE

Ayana Elizabeth Johnson: Marine Biologist and Conservationist

One day in 2019, US marine biologist Ayana Elizabeth Johnson, who proudly calls herself a policy nerd, found herself astonished at something she read. A few weeks before, some members of Congress had pieced together a rough draft for a new environmental bill they hoped to pass. Called the Green New Deal, its goal was to help fight climate change by significantly reducing global emissions of greenhouse gases by 2050. To that end, the bill called for creating several new clean energy industries.

What struck Johnson as strange and disquieting about the synopsis of the bill she read was that it made no mention of the ocean. "My gut reaction," she recalls, "was if this proposal doesn't include the ocean, it's just never going to be enough" to slow climate change enough for humanity to avoid its most dire effects. "Because the ocean is bearing the brunt of a lot of impacts of climate," she continues, "it has absorbed over 90 per cent of the heat that we've trapped with greenhouse gases. It's absorbed about a third of the carbon dioxide we've emitted by burning fossil fuels and this has changed the ocean dramatically."[44]

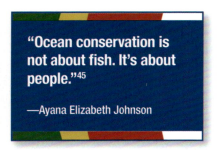

"Ocean conservation is not about fish. It's about people."[45]

—Ayana Elizabeth Johnson

Indeed, Johnson explains, climate change is not a distant threat that perhaps will affect the world close to a century in the future. Rather, it is happening now, and its effects become more dramatic with each passing year. People need to demand that their representatives in Congress act more quickly and forcefully to slow climate change, she says, and they must include ocean conservation in the plan.

Not surprisingly, therefore, reading the overview of the new bill seriously frustrated Johnson, who feels that people's casual reactions to climate change are no less dangerous than climate change itself. "The most important thing I've learned," she states,

> is that ocean conservation is not about fish. It's about people. And it's people who keep me devoted to my mission: figuring out how we can use the ocean without using it up. . . . Overfishing is so extreme that since 1950 we've killed around 90 percent of the world's tuna and sharks. And we're on track to have more plastic than fish in the ocean by 2050. . . . Put simply, we need the ocean.[45]

Falling in Love with the Ocean

Johnson has said on several occasions that her fascination with and love of the ocean began when she was a child. Born in Brooklyn, New York, on August 23, 1980, her first exposure to the sea was limited to her parents occasionally taking her to the beach. When she was five, however, the family moved to Key West, Florida. There, little Ayana went to local beaches far more often, as well as learned to swim. Plus, she was exposed to parts of the wondrous world lying beneath the water's surface. "I went on a glass-bottomed boat," she later remembered, "and I saw a coral reef for the first time. And I realized that there was this whole other universe and I wanted to know everything about it."[46]

The Power of the Ocean

Johnson frequently makes the point that the ocean has certain properties and capacities that can be beneficial to coastal and other areas increasingly suffering from the ravages of climate change. In an article for *Scientific American,* she writes,

> While we might respect the sea's capacity to upend and rend lives and communities, what we have turned our backs on is its power to *heal*. . . . Around 40 percent of Americans live in coastal counties. Imagine if the homes and business along our coasts were powered by offshore wind and waves. . . . Offshore, the wind blows more strongly and consistently than it does over land, so floating turbines could mean more energy, generated more reliably. . . . Offshore wind can and should leap from providing essentially zero percent of our national energy to over 10 percent by 2050 if we are to achieve the needed rapid decarbonization of our electricity grid. And then there's the burgeoning technology for harnessing the energy of waves and currents, and even spreading solar panels across the sea surface. . . . [In addition, coastal] wetlands can hold five times more carbon in their soils than a temperate or tropical forest!

Ayana Elizabeth Johnson, "To Save the Climate, Look to the Oceans," *Observations* (blog), *Scientific American,* June 8, 2020. https://blogs.scientificamerican.com.

At first, the young girl learned about the ocean from her father, who had lived on the Caribbean island of Jamaica as a child. "My dad immigrated to the U.S. when he was in his late twenties, early thirties," she explained in an online interview.

> He grew up fishing, having fish fries on the beach and free diving—all of that. I learned through him a little bit more about the specificity of marine ecosystems, and how much they had changed within his lifetime. Marine ecosystems

of Jamaica just crumbled. Part of my family story is: everything he loved disappeared before his eyes. He stopped going fishing because it was just so depressing. We'd go out miles offshore and still not catch anything. He watched that decline in Jamaica, and then moved to New York, fishing off of Long Island, and experienced the same thing again.[47]

Johnson's initial fascination with the ocean, which had been partially shaped by her father's experiences, continued to grow and soon consumed her thoughts and dreams on a regular basis. "I fell completely in love with the ocean,"[48] she later reminisced. As it turned out, this intense interest in everything having to do with the ocean was not a passing phase, as it tends to be for many young people. "After falling in love with something and then realizing that it's threatened," she says, "of course your reaction is, 'well, what are we going to do about it?'"[49] In her case, the answer to that question seemed clear. Well before she had reached her teen years, she had decided to become a marine biologist.

Learning Science Through Hard Work

Early on, Johnson realized that to make her dream of becoming a marine biologist come true, she would have to attend college. With that goal in mind, she got good grades in high school and, partly for that reason, was accepted to Harvard University. There, she found herself surrounded by other young people who were fascinated by the ocean. She remembers that many of those fellow students were "experienced scuba divers, or who had grown up sailing or as lifeguards at the beach." Also, they too were disturbed at the way humans were polluting the seas. In addition, they shared her worries that the gradual destruction of ocean ecosystems was steadily degrading life for humans, especially those living in coastal regions. Often, she and her classmates shared personal experiences and agreed that at times "you can't have a fish fry on the beach, or the water's too polluted to go swimming with your family and friends." Such things "are not just disruptions to nature," she remarks, "but also disruptions to culture."[50]

Johnson admits that excelling in her studies at Harvard was not an easy task, partly because she felt she lacked a natural ability to absorb difficult scientific concepts. "When I got to college," she explains, "certainly my best grades were not in science and it wasn't the easiest for me." However, she adds, "It was the most interesting." Moreover, she made up for whatever shortcomings she may have had by rigorously applying herself to her studies. "I just really cared," she says. So, her determination to learn the material, even if only for personal satisfaction, drove her onward month after month and year after year. "I'm one of those weirdos," she continues, who studied scientific principles "without ever intending to be a researcher, without ever intending to be an academic or a professor, but I was like, [just for myself] I want to understand this stuff really well."[51]

Maintaining this "can do" attitude, Johnson graduated from Harvard in 2009 with her bachelor's degree in environmental science. Immediately afterward, she enrolled at the prestigious Scripps Institute of Oceanography in San Diego, California, where she majored in marine biology. Her main interest academically was in the quest for ways to sustain and manage the world's endangered coral reefs. But she also addressed topics on which she would later concentrate heavily in her professional research; these included ocean conservation, sustainable fishing, and climate change.

Addressing the Ocean's Fate

After graduating with a PhD from Scripps in 2011, Johnson swiftly made a move that established her reputation as a serious scientist as well as someone who could make a difference in the fate of the ocean. Namely, in 2012 she invented a new type of fish trap. The device greatly reduces "bycatch," which comprises the fish that are unintentionally caught in fishing nets. As Johnson explains,

> Putting vertical, rectangular holes, aka escape gaps, in opposing corners of fish traps can reduce bycatch by up to 80%, without reducing (and potentially even increasing) the value of the catch. How, you ask? Escape gaps allow the narrow-bodied and juvenile fish (including lots of herbivores) to escape, while retaining the larger, meatier fish that fishers want to catch.[52]

Also in 2012, Johnson took a job with the Waitt Institute, a nonprofit organization in Washington, DC, that researches and helps to fund ocean conservation projects. Her rise in the organization proved meteoric, and a year later she was its executive director.

Marine biologist Ayana Elizabeth Johnson (pictured in 2019) has launched or helped to launch many ocean conservation initiatives. These ventures have established her as a leading climate scientist.

Working with Waitt's resources, she co-founded the Blue Halo Initiative, which partnered with local communities and governments in Barbuda and other Caribbean islands. The region's first successful ocean zoning project, it established sanctuaries where fishing was not allowed in hopes of conserving and restoring disappearing local fish populations. The project provides maps, communications devices, and scientific advice to local fishers, economic planners, and government workers. Since its initial implementation, Blue Halo has already generated measurably larger fish and lobster populations, healthier coastal ecosystems, and more lucrative livelihoods for local fishers and merchants.

During the following few years, Johnson launched or helped to launch other similar initiatives relating to ocean conservation. These ventures have established her as a leading climate scientist, one who is respected by colleagues and environmentalists around the globe. "With her expertise, personal story, and collaborative grassroots approach to problem solving," reporter Bonnie Tsui observes, "Johnson has emerged as a uniquely powerful voice in the environmental movement."[53]

One of Johnson's many projects is the Urban Ocean Lab, which is a think tank, or a group of experts who convene to discuss and plan for various future projects. Its goal is to offer solutions to problems that US coastal cities are encountering as a result of climate change and ocean pollution. One of the lab's websites sums up its intent, stating,

> [A third] of Americans (and rising) live in coastal cities. We are unprepared for rising seas and storms, and historically-disadvantaged communities are often hit first and worst. Our safety, economies, food security, and communities are at risk. Urban Ocean Lab cultivates rigorous, creative, equitable, and practical climate and ocean policy, for the future of coastal cities.[54]

> "Johnson has emerged as a uniquely powerful voice in the environmental movement."[53]
>
> —Bonnie Tsui, reporter

How Racism Impedes the Fight Against Climate Change

In a *Washington Post* article, Johnson explains how racism hampers efforts to fight climate change.

> If we want to successfully address climate change, we need people of color. Not just because pursuing diversity is a good thing to do . . . but because, black people are significantly more concerned about climate change than white people (57 percent vs. 49 percent), and Latinx people are even more concerned (70 percent)....
>
> Black Americans who are already committed to working on climate solutions still have to live in America, brutalized by institutions of the state, constantly pummeled with images, words and actions showing just us how many of our fellow citizens do not, in fact, believe that black lives matter. Climate work is hard and heartbreaking as it is. Many people don't feel the urgency, or balk at the initial cost of transitioning our energy infrastructure, without considering the cost of inaction. Many fail to grasp how dependent humanity is on intact ecosystems. When you throw racism and bigotry in the mix, it becomes something near impossible. . . .
>
> Look, I would love to ignore racism and focus all my attention on climate. But I can't. Because I am human. And I'm black. And ignoring racism won't make it go away.

Ayana Elizabeth Johnson, "I'm a Black Climate Expert. Racism Derails Our Efforts to Save the Planet," *Washington Post,* June 3, 2020. www.washingtonpost.com.

The Blue New Deal and Climate Change

Another similar initiative that Johnson championed was the so-called Blue New Deal, which began in earnest in 2020. It was born in part as a reaction to the absence of ocean-related themes in the Green New Deal proposed in Congress the year before.

"What I thought of when I saw this congressional resolution was that they're leaving out a lot of solutions," she recalls. It was not just that the Green New Deal failed to plan for saving the ocean, she explains, but its approach also failed to consider the many ways in which the ocean could help save the planet as a whole. For example, coastal ecosystems, such as mangroves, can absorb close to five times more carbon dioxide from the air than land-based forests. Other benefits of the ocean, she states, include energy generated by the tides, huge offshore wind turbines, and floating solar panels. Likewise, potentially massive seaweed farms can provide a large-scale source of protein for domestic animals and people too. "You don't need to feed [these things]," she points out, and they can "provide a lot of jobs."[55]

A large part of the Blue New Deal's thrust is aimed at combating climate change. The accelerating warming of the planet's atmosphere and the ocean is already altering weather systems; increasing the frequency and intensity of storms, forest fires, and major flooding events; and destroying the globe's coral reefs and other coastal ecosystems. Johnson contends that climate change is the single biggest threat that the ocean—and, by extension, the planet—now faces. In a 2019 TED talk, she described the effects of changing climate on coral reefs:

> Because of climate change, on top of overfishing and pollution, coral reefs may be gone within thirty years, an entire ecosystem erased. This is devastating because hundreds of millions of people around the world depend on reefs for their nutrition and income. Let that sink in. A little bit of good news is that places like Belize [and] Barbuda . . . are protecting the reefs. Also, more and more places are establishing protected areas that protect the entire ecosystem. These are critical efforts. But it's not enough. As I stand here today, only 2.2 percent of the ocean is protected. . . . We're in the midst of the sixth mass extinction and we, humans, are causing it.[56]

Marine biologists and climate scientists around the world agree that Johnson, who turned forty-two in 2022, appears to have a long and bright future ahead of her. In part, they point out, this is because she has a particularly engaging manner. "Ayana is genuinely funny," says Alex Blumberg, cofounder of Gimlet Media. "She's an actual subject-matter expert who's charismatic and can crack a joke and think on her feet. That's rare."[57]

When asked what she wants to accomplish in that future, Johnson consistently repeats that her goal remains the same as it was when she was a child: to save the ocean and sustain it for later generations. She also emphasizes that to achieve that lofty goal, humanity must act quickly. "We absolutely can't wait until everyone 100 per cent agrees on everything," she warns, "because we'd never get anything done." And it absolutely must be done, she adds. Ultimately, humans cannot survive without a healthy ocean, so "we *have* to restore and protect [it]."[58]

SOURCE NOTES

Introduction: Standing on the Shoulders of Giants
1. Quoted in Live Science Staff, "Amazing Black Scientists," June 10, 2020. www.livescience.com.
2. Cindy Shmerler, "Overlooked No More: Rebecca Lee Crumpler, Who Battled Prejudice in Medicine." July 17, 2021. www.nytimes.com.
3. Quoted in Christopher Rosen, "Neil deGrasse Tyson: B.o.B. Claims Debunked on Nightly Show," *Entertainment Weekly,* January 28, 2016. https://ew.com.

Chapter One
George Washington Carver: Agriculturalist and Inventor
4. Quoted in Mark D. Hersey, *My Work Is That of Conservation: An Environmental Biography of George Washington Carver.* Athens: University of Georgia Press, 2011, p. 163.
5. Linda O. McMurry, *George Washington Carver: Scientist and Symbol.* New York: Oxford University Press, 1981, p. 171.
6. Quoted in National Park Service, "George Washington Carver National Monument, Missouri." www.nps.gov.
7. Quoted in National Park Service, "George Washington Carver National Monument, Missouri."
8. Wendi Williams, "The Jesup Wagon: Rooted in History, Still Used Today," *Business & Community* (blog), Alabama Cooperative Extension System, February 6, 2020. www.aces.edu.
9. Quoted in Today in Science History, "Science Quotes by George Washington Carver." https://todayinsci.com.
10. Editors of History.com, "George Washington Carver Begins Experimental Project with Henry Ford," July 16, 2020. www.history.com.
11. Quoted in Hersey, *My Work Is That of Conservation,* p. 167.
12. Quoted in Gary Kremer, *George Washington Carver: In His Own Words.* Columbia: University of Missouri Press, 1987, p. 136.

13. Quoted in John Hyde "George Washington Carver," *Iowa Pathways,* Iowa Public Broadcasting Service. www.iowapbs.org.
14. Quoted in National Park Service History Library, "George Washington Carver." http://npshistory.com.

Chapter Two
Percy L. Julian: Chemist and College Professor
15. Quoted in *NOVA*, "Julian Speaks," Public Broadcasting Service, 2007. www.pbs.org.
16. American Chemical Society National Historic Chemica Landmarks, "Percy Julian: Synthesis of Physostigmine." www.acs.org.
17. Quoted in *NOVA*, "Forgotten Genius," Public Broadcasting Service, February 6, 2007. www.pbs.org.
18. Quoted in *NOVA,* "Forgotten Genius."
19. Quoted in *NOVA,* "Forgotten Genius."
20. Quoted in *NOVA,* "Forgotten Genius."
21. Quoted in *NOVA,* "Forgotten Genius."
22. Quoted in *NOVA,* "Forgotten Genius."

Chapter Three
Mae C. Jemison: Physician and Astronaut
23. Mae Jemison, *Find Where the Wind Goes: Moments from My Life.* New York: Scholastic, 2001.
24. Jemison, *Find Where the Wind Goes,* p. 172.
25. Jemison, *Find Where the Wind Goes,* p. 174.
26. Quoted in *Quantum of Science* (blog), "Mae Jemison: The Real Uhura," 2020. https://quantumofjk.blogspot.com.
27. Jemison, *Find Where the Wind Goes,* pp. 11, 13.
28. Jemison, *Find Where the Wind Goes,* p. 47.
29. Jemison, *Find Where the Wind Goes,* p. 189.
30. Jesse Katz, "Shooting Star: Former Astronaut Mae Jemison Brings Her Message Down to Earth," *Stanford Today,* July/August 1996, p. 39.
31. Quoted in Scholastic, "Dr. Mae Jemison Interview," March 15, 2001. https://teacher.scholastic.com.
32. Jemison, *Find Where the Wind Goes,* p. x.
33. Jemison, *Find Where the Wind Goes,* p. 193.
34. Quoted in Doug Erickson, "Astronaut Mae Jemison Inspires a New Generation of Trailblazers," University of Wisconsin–Madison, January 22, 2020. https://news.wisc.edu.

Chapter Four
Neil deGrasse Tyson: Astrophysicist and Science Explainer

35. Neil deGrasse Tyson, *The Sky Is Not the Limit.* New York: Doubleday, 2000, p. 3.
36. Tyson, *The Sky Is Not the Limit,* p. 4.
37. Tyson, *The Sky Is Not the Limit,* p. 13.
38. Tyson, *The Sky Is Not the Limit,* p. 128.
39. Tyson, *The Sky Is Not the Limit,* pp. 36–37.
40. Quoted in Rose Cahalan, "Star Power," *Alcalde*, February 28, 2012. https://alcalde.texasexes.org.
41. Quoted in *NOVA Origins,* "A Conversation with Neil deGrasse Tyson," Public Broadcasting Service, 2004. www.pbs.org.
42. Quoted in Carl Zimmer, "King of the Cosmos," 2012. https://carlzimmer.com.
43. Tyson, *The Sky Is Not the Limit,* pp. 183–84.

Chapter Five
Ayana Elizabeth Johnson: Marine Biologist and Conservationist

44. Quoted in Diane Nazaroff, "How a Scientist Made Sure the Oceans Weren't Forgotten," UNSW Sydney Newsroom, August 23, 2021. https://newsroom.unsw.edu.au.
45. Ayana Elizabeth Johnson, "How to Use the Ocean Without Using It Up," TED Conferences, July 2016. www.ted.com.
46. Quoted in Nazaroff, "How a Scientist Made Sure the Oceans Weren't Forgotten."
47. Quoted in Dawn Lippert, "Fellows Friday: Ayana Elizabeth Johnson," Emerson Collective. www.emersoncollective.com.
48. Johnson, "How to Use the Ocean Without Using It Up."
49. Quoted in Nazaroff, "How a Scientist Made Sure the Oceans Weren't Forgotten."
50. Quoted in Nazaroff, "How a Scientist Made Sure the Oceans Weren't Forgotten."
51. Quoted in Nazaroff, "How a Scientist Made Sure the Oceans Weren't Forgotten."
52. Ayana Elizabeth Johnson, "Solution: Escape Gaps for Fish Traps," May 7, 2013. www.ayanaelizabeth.com.
53. Bonnie Tsui, "Ayana Elizabeth Johnson Is the Climate Leader We Need," Outside, October 31, 2020. www.outsideonline.com.

54. Urban Ocean Lab, homepage. https://urbanoceanlab.org.
55. Quoted in Nazaroff, "How a Scientist Made Sure the Oceans Weren't Forgotten."
56. Ayana Elizabeth Johnson, "A Love Story for the Coral Reef Crisis," TED Conferences, April 2019. www.ted.com.
57. Quoted in Tsui, "Ayana Elizabeth Johnson Is the Climate Leader We Need."
58. Quoted in Nazaroff, "How a Scientist Made Sure the Oceans Weren't Forgotten."

FOR FURTHER RESEARCH

Books

Gene Barretta, *The Secret Garden of George Washington Carver.* New York: Katherine Tegan, 2020.

Michael A. Carson, *African-American Inventions That Changed the World: Influential Inventors and Their Revolutionary Creations*. Grayson, GA: Double Infinity, 2017.

Tammy Gagne, *Forgotten Americans Who Made History.* Mankato, MN: 12-Story Library, 2019.

Dr. Mae Jemison, *Find Where the Wind Goes: Moments from My Life*. Houston, TX: Signal Hill Road, 2021.

Ayana Elizabeth Johnson and Katharine K. Wilkinson, eds., *All We Can Save: Truth, Courage, and Solutions for the Climate Crisis*. London: One World, 2021.

Michelle Lord, *Patricia's Vision: The Doctor Who Saved Sight*. New York: Sterling, 2020.

Pam Pollack and Meg Belvisio, *Who Is Neil deGrasse Tyson?* New York: Penguin Workshop, 2021.

Neil deGrasse Tyson, *Letters from an Astrophysicist.* New York: Norton, 2019.

Internet Sources

Tim Ferriss, "Neil deGrasse Tyson—How to Dream Big, Think Scientifically, and Get More Done (#389)," *Tim Ferriss Show* (blog), October 3, 2019. https://tim.blog.

Virginia Gewin, "What Black Scientists Want from Colleagues and Their Institutions," *Nature,* June 22, 2020. www.nature.com.

Ron Grossman, "Chemist Percy Julian Pushed Past Racial Barriers amid Attacks on His Oak Park Home," *Chicago Tribune,* February 15, 2019. www.chicagotribune.com.

Eric Herschthal, "Black Americans Have Always Understood Science as a Tool in Their Freedom Struggle," *Washington Post,* May 18, 2021. www.washingtonpost.com.

Ayana Elizabeth Johnson, "I'm a Black Climate Expert. Racism Derails Our Efforts to Save the Planet," *Washington Post,* June 3, 2020. www.washingtonpost.com.

Quantum of Science (blog), "Mae Jemison: The Real Uhura," 2020. https://quantumofjk.blogspot.com.

Ella Riley-Adams, "A New Climate Podcast Asks 'Are We Screwed?' — but Still Finds Ways to Be Constructive," *Vogue,* September 18, 2020. www.vogue.com.

Manoush Zomorodi et al., "Ayana Elizabeth Johnson: What Should You Look for When Shopping for Seafood?," *TED Radio Hour*, National Public Radio, June 25, 2021. www.npr.org.

Websites

National Aeronautics and Space Administration (NASA)
www.nasa.gov
This informative NASA website provides very readable biographies of astronauts present and past, including Mae C. Jemison, the first Black female astronaut. The site also describes present and future space station missions, as well as information on how astronauts are selected for their important roles in space exploration.

National Museum of African American History & Culture
https://nmaahc.si.edu
The museum's website directs visitors to all sorts of useful information, including recent news about and upcoming events in the African American community. The site also has descriptions of notable Black Americans, among them the great African American agriculturalist George Washington Carver and noted Black chemist Percy Julian.

Tuskegee University, The Legacy of Dr. George Washington Carver
https://www.tuskegee.edu
This private, historically Black university maintains a large amount of information about Black American inventor George Washington Carver. Links on the university website provide users with information about Carver's life, lists of the peanut-related and other foodstuffs he experimented with, and also some of his personal writings.

INDEX

Note: Boldface page numbers indicate illustrations.

Aer-O-Foam, 23
Amendola, Robert, 17
American Chemical Society, 18
Astrophysics for People in a Hurry (Neil deGrasse Tyson), 44
Azimov, Isaac, 42

Ball, Alice A., 7
Banneker, Benjamin, 4–5
Bash, Frank N., 40
Blue Halo Initiative, 51
Blue New Deal, 52–53
Blumberg, Alex, 54
A Book of Medical Discourses (Crumpler), 5
A Brief Welcome to the Universe (Tyson), 44
Burton, Levar, 31
Bush, George W., 42

Calabar bean, 21
Carver, George Washington, 8–17, **11**
  birth/early life of, 9–10
  death of, 16
  education, 10–12
  as inventor, 14–15
  legacy of, 16–17
  monument honoring, 17
  as teacher, 13
  work toward racial equality, 15–16

Carver, Mary, 10
Carver, Moses, 10, 17
Carver, Susan, 10, 17
Cheyney University, 5
climate change, 45–46
  impact of racism on fight against, 52
  impact on coral reefs, 53
cortisone, 24–25
Corwin, Audrey, 17
Cosmos: A Spacetime Odyssey (TV program), 43–44
Crumpler, Rebecca Lee, 5–6

Dawkins, Richard, 43
Drew, Charles, 7

Endeavour (space shuttle), 34

Fisk University, 20
Ford, Henry, 14–15
400 Years of the Telescope (documentary), 42
Freeman, Morgan, 43

George Washington Carver National Monument (MO), 17
Green New Deal, 45, 52–53

Henson, Matthew, 7
Hess, Fred, 38–39
Howard University, 20
How William Shatner Changed the World (documentary), 31

Jefferson, Thomas, 4
Jemison, Mae C., 7, 27–35, **32**
  birth/early life of, 28–29
  chosen as first Black female astronaut, 33–34
  education, 30–32
  post-NASA career, 34–35
Jesup Agricultural Wagon, 13
Jim Crow, 20
Johnson, Ayana Elizabeth, 45–54, **50**
  birth/early life of, 46–48
  education, 48–49
  on impact of climate change on coral reefs, 53
  on the power of the ocean, 47
  on racism as impediment on fight against climate change, 52
Julian, Anna Roselle, 21
Julian, Percy Lavon, 18–26, **22**
  accomplishments of, 26
  birth/early life of, 19–20
  on growing up under Jim Crow, 20
  on work with soybean protein, 25
Julian Laboratories, 25, 26

Katz, Jesse, 33–34

Letters from an Astrophysicist (Neil deGrasse Tyson), 44

National Aeronautics and Space Administration (NASA), 60
National Museum of African American History & Culture, 60
Natural History (magazine), 41
Newton, Isaac, 7
Nichols, Nichelle, 28
NOVA (TV program), 43

O'Brien, William J., 23
Origins (TV miniseries), 42

peanuts, 8
  oil from, as polio treatment, 12
  uses of, 9, 14
Perry, Robert, 7
Petsko, Gregory, 26
physostigmine, 21–22, 26
Pikl, Josef, 21
Plotz, Charles, 24
Prady, Bill, 44
progesterone, 19
Provident Hospital, **6**, 6–7

racism, 6
  Carver's efforts against, 15–16
  impact on fight against climate change, 52
  Percy Julian and, 20, 22, 26
Ride, Sally, 33
Rivers, Joan, 43
Roosevelt, Franklin D., 12

Sagan, Carl, 39, 42
Scientific American (magazine), 47
Shmerler, Cindy, 6
Simpson College, 12
The Sky Is Not the Limit (Neil deGrasse Tyson), 44
StarTalk Radio (talk show), 42
Star Trek (TV program), 27, 31
sterols, 19

Takei, George, 43
testosterone, 19
Truman, Harry S., 16, 17
Tsui, Bonnie, 51
Tuskegee University, 8, 13, 60
Tyson, Cyril deGrasse, 37

Tyson, Neil deGrasse, 7, 36–44, **41**
    as author, 44
    on belief as inapplicable to science, 38
    birth/early life of, 37–39
    on first exposure to astronomy, 36–37
    joins staff of Hayden Planetarium, 41–42
    on science as multidisciplinary, 43
Tyson, Sunchita M., 37

Urban Ocean Lab, 51
USS *George Washington Carver* (submarine), 16

Waitt Institute, 50
Washington, Booker T., 13, 16
Washington, George, 4
Washington Post (newspaper), 52
Weathersby, Coty, 35
Williams, Daniel Hale, 6–7
Woods, Granville, 7

PICTURE CREDITS

Cover: Space Prime/Alamy Stock Photo

6: Bridgeman Images
11: World History Archive/Alamy Stock Photo
22: Science History Images/Alamy Stock Photo
32: stock imagery/Alamy Stock Photo
41: Abaca Press/Alamy Stock Photo
50: ZUMA Press, Inc./Alamy Stock Photo

ABOUT THE AUTHOR

Classical historian, amateur astronomer, and award-winning author Don Nardo has written numerous volumes about scientific topics, including *Destined for Space,* winner of the Eugene M. Emme Award for best astronomical literature; *Tycho Brahe,* winner of the National Science Teaching Association's best book of the year; *Planet Under Siege: Climate Change; Deadliest Dinosaurs;* and *The History of Science.* Nardo, who also composes and arranges orchestral music, lives with his wife, Christine, in Massachusetts.